004688

KU-009-243

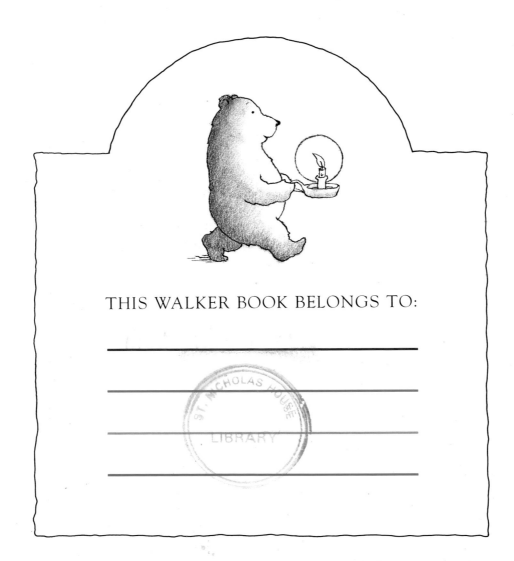

THIS WALKER BOOK BELONGS TO:

ST. NICHOLAS HOUSE

LIBRARY

Spotted English

Orange Rex

Rex

Belgian Hare   Netherland Dwarf   Flemish Giant

To Ben

With thanks to John Barker, B. Vet. Med., M.R.C.V.S.

First published 1995 by
Walker Books Ltd, 87 Vauxhall Walk
London SE11 5HJ

This edition published 1996

2 4 6 8 10 9 7 5 3

© 1995 Colin and Jacqui Hawkins

This book has been typeset in Monotype Garamond.

Printed in Hong Kong

British Library Cataloguing in Publication Data
A catalogue record for this book is
available from the British Library.

ISBN 0-7445-4380-0

How to Look After Your
RABBIT

Colin and Jacqui Hawkins

WALKER BOOKS

AND SUBSIDIARIES

LONDON · BOSTON · SYDNEY

Rabbit History

Rabbits originally lived in northern Europe but were forced to move south during the Ice Age.

The Common European rabbit is the ancestor of our domestic breeds and is native to Spain.

The Romans introduced rabbits to France and other parts of Europe, including Britain.

In the Middle Ages French monks bred rabbits for food. They were probably responsible for many of the different breeds we have today.

Rabbits were left in Australia by explorers, who kept them aboard their ships as a fresh supply of meat. At one time there were so many wild rabbits in Australia the farmers had to treat them as pests.

Choosing Your Rabbit

Choose a rabbit that looks lively and healthy. Check that her teeth are clean and her claws short.

alert, clean ears

dry, twitching nose

I'm a bonny bunny.

firm back

sleek, shiny coat

The female rabbit is called a "doe" and the male a "buck". Rabbits are sociable animals and you may want to keep more than one. If you do, try to get two does from the same litter.

Do not choose a rabbit that has diarrhoea ...

and avoid one that sneezes and has a runny nose.

It is best to buy a rabbit in spring when it is between nine and twelve weeks old.

Rabbits are clean and gentle and can live for over five years, but like all pets they need care and attention. Make sure you have time to look after a rabbit before you get one.

Home Sweet Home

Baby rabbits can grow into big adults, so it is a good idea to buy or make the largest hutch you can.

backwards-sloping roof covered with tarred felt

weather-proofed sides

What a hutch!

separate sleeping area

ramp

legs to raise hutch away from damp and vermin

Zzzzzzzzzzzzz

Make sure the sleeping compartment is lined with absorbent material such as peat or cat litter. Put straw on top for your pet to snuggle into.

Hey man, *turn the hutch! Turn the hutch!*

It is better to keep a hutch in a shed than outside, but if your rabbit has to be outdoors, make sure the hutch is in a sheltered place, away from the wind and out of the sun. Rabbits can suffer from heatstroke and the cold.

Brr! It's freezing in here.

There should be strong wire netting on the front of the living area of the hutch so that you can see your pet and she can see you. Make sure the door of the hutch fastens securely.

I can see you.

How to Feed Your Rabbit

Whee! Plastic dishes make excellent Frisbees.

Make sure your rabbit's food bowl is too heavy for her to tip over. Do not use a plastic bowl. Your pet might gnaw it and hurt herself on the broken pieces.

Mmm! I just love water.

A drip-fed water bottle with a stainless steel spout is the safest and cleanest way of giving your pet fresh water.

Anyone for stick?

Keep a small piece of wood in the hutch for your rabbit to gnaw on. This will stop her teeth growing too long.

A salt lick attached to the bars of the cage will provide her with the extra mineral salts she needs.

A little hayrack stops hay getting trampled on the floor.

Feed your pet two small meals a day and don't put out too much food as rabbits can get very fat.

A rabbit will quickly get used to a regular feeding routine, so try and feed your pet at the same times each day.

What to Feed Your Rabbit

Rabbits are herbivores, which means they only eat plants. Eating is the main pastime of a domestic rabbit, so make sure yours always has interesting food.

Dry food pellets are full of nutrition but do not alone make a very interesting or healthy diet. They will also make your pet thirsty.

Bran mash with a little hot water or milk makes an excellent breakfast.

Slurp! Slurp!

In the evening give your rabbit fresh greens such as lettuce, cabbage, spinach or watercress. Leave her a carrot to gnaw on two or three times a week.

Many rabbits also enjoy fresh fruit such as apples, pears, tomatoes and even a slice of melon from time to time.

You can also feed her washed weeds from your garden, such as dandelion leaves, clover and chickweed. She will leave anything she doesn't like.

Yuk!

I'll have cabbage, sprouts and lettuce.

MENU

Hay is a very important part of a rabbit's daily diet, so fill the hayrack each morning and evening.

Exercise

Like all animals, rabbits need exercise to stay fit and healthy, and an outdoor run is an excellent place for your pet to play and nibble grass in safety.

This type of run is called an ark and can be made or bought. Make sure you put it in the shade and always attach a water bottle to the outside. Move the ark every day so that the rabbit has fresh grass to nibble and never put it on grass that has been treated with weedkiller.

An ark should have a shelter at one end and wire netting on the bottom to stop your pet burrowing out and other animals, such as foxes, from digging in.

Make sure your rabbit is not bothered by other pets ...

and don't leave her in the run at night or in bad weather.

Even if she has been nibbling grass all day, you should still give your pet the usual amount of food at her regular feeding time.

Rabbit Hygiene

Help your rabbit stay healthy and happy by keeping her hutch clean.

Remember, a clean hutch is a happy hutch.

I'll make a clean sweep of this.

Every day, sweep up unwanted food scraps and replace soggy straw in the sleeping area. Clean the food bowl and rinse and fill the water bottle.

What a good girl I am.

Rabbits are naturally very clean animals and some will learn to use a metal tray as a toilet, but be sure to place it well away from the food.

Give the hutch a thorough clean once a week with hot soapy water and use a scraper to clean right into the corners. Rinse soap away, spray with mild disinfectant and leave the hutch to dry.

After cleaning, put fresh peat and straw in the sleeping area and shavings or paper on the main floor.

Handling and Holding

Always be gentle with rabbits. They are shy animals but can easily be tamed if handled with love and care. Remember when choosing your pet that smaller breeds are easier to hold when fully grown.

This is nice.

OW!

Never pick up your rabbit by the ears. It hurts!

Use both hands – one to hold her by the scruff of the neck and the other to support her bottom.

Gently now.

Scoop her up and hold her close against your chest.

Hold her firmly and if she starts to struggle put her down. She could hurt you or herself if she kicks too hard with her strong back legs. Cradle your rabbit in your arms or let her lie with her head over one shoulder.

Is this a bunny hug?

Lettice!

I hate that name.

Talk to your pet. She may eventually learn her name.

You're so sweet I've just got to give you a lick.

As your rabbit gets to know you she will become very tame and if she really likes you she will lick you.

Grooming

Rabbits are clean animals and groom themselves regularly, using their paws to wash their faces with spit. They also use their teeth as a comb to pick dirt out of their fur.

This is *the way* we wash our fur, wash our fur, wash our fur...

This is the way we brush our fur, on a cold and frosty morning.

If you have a long-haired variety, such as an Angora, you must brush your pet every day. Other types of rabbit will also enjoy the attention, especially in the spring when they shed their winter fur. Start at the head and brush gently in the direction the fur grows.

When grooming, check your pet for fleas and dust with insecticide powder if necessary.

If your rabbit's claws grow very long they should be clipped by the vet.

When you go away on holiday remember to arrange for someone to come and give your pet food and water each day, or if you prefer you could board her out with a vet or pet shop.

I want to be alone.

Healthcare

If your rabbit huddles in the corner of her hutch she may be feeling ill.

Other signs of ill-health are not eating and a dull, untidy coat. Take your rabbit to the vet immediately if you are worried.

I just can't be bothered.

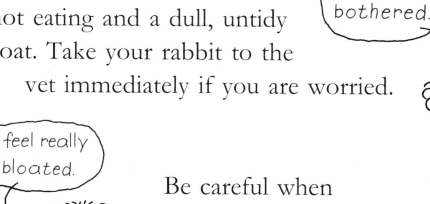

I feel really bloated.

Be careful when feeding your rabbit green leaves – too much young greenstuff can cause diarrhoea and wet greens might make her stomach swell up with bloat. This is uncomfortable for rabbits as they cannot bring up wind.

Snuffles is a serious rabbit disease that affects the breathing and can lead to pneumonia. If you notice your rabbit sneezing take her to the vet as soon as possible.

Do not be alarmed if you see your rabbit eating her own droppings. Don't try and stop her. This is a vital part of her digestive system and rabbits can die if they are not allowed to do it.

Having Babies

You should think carefully whether you want your rabbit to breed. Bear in mind that you will need to find good homes for all the babies and there may be as many as eight in a litter.

This hutch ain't big enough for the both of us.

The male and female should be introduced in the buck's hutch. The female might attack a strange male in her own home.

A doe is pregnant for about thirty days. During this time she should be handled as little as possible and given plenty to eat. About a week before the babies are due she will start pulling her fur out to line her nest.

Just a little bit more.

The doe can manage the birth without any help, just make sure she and the family remain undisturbed for at least a day after the babies are born. The male rabbits will not help look after the babies.

Baby rabbits are born deaf, blind and without fur or teeth. The mother will look after them, but they grow very quickly and at nine weeks are able to look after themselves and go to their new homes.

Rabbits Indoors

If your pet lives indoors she will need her own cosy sleeping box lined with hay, where she can rest at any time.

A rabbit makes a very good indoor pet and can be trained to use a litter tray. You can use ordinary cat litter.

I really like living indoors.

carrot juice

toast

comfy chair

Do you mind! This is a private poo!

If your rabbit is used to living in the house be careful that she doesn't escape when you open an outside door. She may never come back!

Watch out that your rabbit does not nibble through wires; she could get an electric shock. Pet shops sell a spray which you can use to coat any visible wires. It tastes unpleasant and will stop unwanted nibbling.

You're my best buddy, bunny!

Your rabbit may eventually become friends with other pets such as dogs and cats, but they should be introduced gradually and and you may have to be patient.

Lop-eared   Dutch

English

Mini Rex

Angora

MORE WALKER PAPERBACKS
For You to Enjoy

Also by Colin & Jacqui Hawkins
HOW TO LOOK AFTER YOUR...

Four brilliant pet-care books, packed with information for the young, would-be pet owner.

"A must... There are useful tips on home, feeding, health
and much more with fun drawings." *R.S.P.C.A. Animal Action*

How to Look After Your Cat   0-7445-4737-7
How to Look After Your Dog   0-7445-4738-5
How to Look After Your Hamster   0-7445-4379-7
How to Look After Your Rabbit   0-7445-4380-0
£4.50 each

COME FOR A RIDE ON THE GHOST TRAIN

"Every page must be turned with care as a comic, but wholly
scary surprise is revealed under the simplest flaps. Irresistible."
Julia Eccleshare, The Bookseller

0-7445-3671-5   £4.99

TERRIBLE TERRIBLE TIGER/THE WIZARD'S CAT

Two wonderfully entertaining rhyming picture books about a tiger
who is not quite what he seems and a cat who wishes he were something else!

Terrible Terrible Tiger   0-7445-5230-3   £4.50
The Wizard's Cat   0-7445-5231-1   £4.50

Walker Paperbacks are available from most booksellers, or by post from B.B.C.S., P.O. Box 941, Hull, North Humberside HU1 3YQ
24 hour telephone credit card line 01482 224626

To order, send: Title, author, ISBN number and price for each book ordered, your full name and address,
cheque or postal order payable to BBCS for the total amount and allow the following for postage and packing:
UK and BFPO: £1.00 for the first book, and 50p for each additional book to a maximum of £3.50.
Overseas and Eire: £2.00 for the first book, £1.00 for the second and 50p for each additional book

Prices and availability are subject to change without notice.